Accepting Ourselves

Veronica Ray

About Hazelden Publishing

As part of the Hazelden Betty Ford Foundation, Hazelden Publishing offers both cutting-edge educational resources and inspirational books. Our print and digital works help guide individuals in treatment and recovery, and their loved ones. Professionals who work to prevent and treat addiction also turn to Hazelden Publishing for evidence-based curricula, digital content solutions, and videos for use in schools, treatment programs, correctional programs, and electronic health records systems. We also offer training for implementation of our curricula.

Through published and digital works, Hazelden Publishing extends the reach of healing and hope to individuals, families, and communities affected by addiction and related issues.

For more information about
Hazelden publications,
please call **800-328-9000**
or visit us online at
hazelden.org/bookstore

INTRODUCTION

To accept something is to receive it willingly—without white knuckles or clenched teeth.

—Earnie Larsen and
Carol Larsen Hegarty from
Days of Healing, Days of Joy

Accepting ourselves and others means finding serenity in our relationships. In accepting others, we accept what we cannot change or control. In accepting ourselves, we discover and take responsibility for what we can change. Facing people and relationships realistically, we grow in trust, forgiveness, maturity, tolerance, and faith. We discover our similarities and learn to accept our differences without feeling threatened.

By accepting the realities of ourselves and others, we can open the door to caring, sharing, and living in harmony. We can take care of ourselves and allow others to do the same. True acceptance brings relief from futile struggles and unrealistic expectations and fantasies. We learn to see ourselves and others as we truly are. We learn to see the spirit beneath the body, ego, and behavior. We begin learning to understand, accept, and love ourselves and others as our Higher Power does.

In the light of reality, we replace our desire for control with serenity. We learn not only to survive despite ourselves and others, but to embrace our humanity. We move beyond merely putting up with reality because we have no choice, to accepting it, "without white knuckles or clenched teeth." We learn to live in health, peace, and harmony with ourselves and all people. Through love and forgiveness, we find true peace of mind.

Trust

Trusting people may be difficult if we feel we have been betrayed in the past. We may close ourselves off from sharing with others at all. We may harbor suspicions that everyone will eventually betray us. We may grow frustrated and lonely in our lack of trust, and suddenly place great trust in someone we hardly know.

Healthy trust is a matter of balance. We don't give all our trust away recklessly, nor do we refuse to trust anyone, ever. Trust grows with time and experience in a relationship.

Trusting others is built on self-trust. If we respect and honor ourselves, recognize our options, and take responsibility for our choices, then we can trust ourselves. Knowing that we will take care of ourselves enables us to trust others in a healthy way.

Trusting myself and my Higher Power helps me know when and how much to trust others.

Gratitude

Everyone we've ever met or known has served a purpose in our lives. Some have given us experiences through which we learned valuable lessons. Some have led us toward our recovery. Some have fulfilled a purpose we can't yet see, and perhaps never will.

We can be thankful for everyone who touches our lives. They were sent by our Higher Power. They guide us along our journey of spiritual evolution. They provide us with opportunities to learn, teach, love, forgive, accept, let go, change, and grow. They are essential to our never-ending development.

Our gratitude can be expressed in many ways. We can thank others directly, in words or kind actions. We can send the entire universe our gratitude in prayer. We can keep working on our spiritual growth, touching other lives with love.

I thank God for all the people who have touched my life.

Judgments

How do we see others? Do we judge them according to standards of our culture or family? Do we see them as they see themselves?

God sees us all in the light of perfect understanding and forgiveness. God's love is not modulated by judgments of us. We can never lose God's love for us. We can only lose our awareness of it by judging and condemning.

In judging others, we judge ourselves. In seeing only the surfaces of others, and not their spiritual centers, we can see only the surfaces of ourselves. The part of us that judges is not the spiritual part that connects us to our Higher Power.

We cannot attain the perfection of God in this life. But we can let go of our judgments and let God show us our own and others' true selves.

I release my judgments of others.

No Two Are Alike

Like snowflakes, no two people are exactly alike. We are all different in various ways. We have different abilities, interests, strengths and weaknesses, desires, backgrounds, opportunities, passions, and points of view. Some of us love football and others prefer baseball. Some of us play the stock market while others play bingo.

But none of these differences threatens who we are. We don't need to persuade others to agree with our point of view. We don't need to be like everyone else any more than leaves or snowflakes or grains of sand need to be the same.

Our Higher Power makes no distinctions between us. We are all human beings, with bodies, minds, emotions, and spirits. We each follow our own path, fulfilling our own purpose.

I respectfully accept the differences between myself and others.

Acceptance

Sometimes we try to form a healthy, loving relationship with someone, but it doesn't seem to work. We may be there when they need us to listen or support them in their struggles. We may call them, visit them, write to them, and send them encouraging words or gifts.

We may do all this and more, in a healthy, loving way, and yet receive no response or reciprocation. They may not be there for us as we are for them. They may not initiate contact with us, even if they seem happy to hear from us when we call. Even if they do seem to appreciate our efforts and want a relationship with us, they may not meet us halfway.

We can choose whether or not to continue our behavior or end the relationship. Either way, we can accept and respect their choices.

I accept other people as they are.

Conflict

It may seem as if others impede our happiness, health, and peace of mind. We may think that if only others would do this or stop doing that, everything would be great. And so we are always in conflict with others because they don't think, feel, or act as we wish.

Dr. Gerald G. Jampolsky writes in *Goodbye To Guilt*, "All the conflicting interactions we have with other people, regardless of their forms, are simply variations on the game of guilt." We make others guilty to make ourselves innocent. We make others wrong to make ourselves right.

When we let go of judging everyone as guilty or innocent, right or wrong, we can accept our differences. Happiness doesn't come from seeing ourselves as right and others as wrong. It comes from valuing mutual respect and harmony over conflict.

I let go of conflict and seek true happiness in harmony with others.

Ending Relationships

It is a fact of life that, for various reasons, relationships sometimes end. This is painful for us as long as we cling to memories of what was or fantasies of what might have been.

But both memories and fantasies exist only in our imaginations. In reality, people and relationships change. If someone chooses to leave us or to continue unhealthy behavior, we must leave for our own well-being, and the relationship ends. We can't control the person's leaving or his or her behavior. We can accept it.

We can let go of wishing things were different, and accept reality. We can learn whatever lessons the relationship holds for us and move on. Releasing the other person and the relationship also releases us to grow in new ways.

I accept the changing nature of my relationships.

Many Roads

We meet many people in our lives, all with different stories to tell about where they've been. We may pass some of the same markers, or cover similar terrain, but no two of us ever travel exactly the same road.

Some may join us for a little while, but then turn in another direction. We may pass each other at intersections. Some roads may look harder than others, with rocks and pitfalls in the way. Other roads may look smooth and straight. But each road has its purpose and destination.

As we move forward, we can remember that the roads of life are many. Our way may not be the way for others. Even if we think we have found a better road to travel, we can't direct others to follow us. They each have their own route to follow, and none of us is the Mapmaker.

With our Higher Power's help, we each follow our own road.

Expectations

When we expect others to think, feel, or act in certain ways, we set ourselves up for disappointment. Our expectations have nothing to do with who other people really are, but rather reflect who we are and what we want.

When others don't live up to our expectations, we often become angry with them. They've disrupted our plans, disturbed our view of them and our world. Expectations close off our ability to let others be themselves and to see them as they are.

If we let go of our expectations and allow others to be themselves, our relationships can grow. We can discover each other as we really are. Free of expectations and judgments, we can be open to pleasant surprises. Others may not be whatever we expect them to be. They may be even better.

I let go of all my expectations of others. They are free to be themselves.

Mirrors

Letting go of our judgments of and reactions to the people in our lives, we can see them more clearly. We can let others serve as mirrors through which we can learn and grow.

Everyone in our lives reflects some part of us. If others treat us with anger, impatience, or disregard, perhaps it reflects the way we treat ourselves or others. At the same time, if someone treats us with love and respect, we can only see and accept it if we love and respect ourselves. The kindness, love, beauty, and peacefulness we observe is a reflection of those qualities in us.

As we grow and change, we may notice that others seem to change. As we become more patient, serene, and loving, so do they. Others mirror our positive changes and the world looks better and better.

I am open to learning about myself through observing others.

Assumptions

What do we think we know about other people? Do we see people's faces and decide we know exactly what they're thinking or feeling? Do we see strangers and assume they think, act, and live a certain way based on how they're dressed? Do we assume that the people we see every day are showing us all there is to know about them?

We often make even more assumptions about people close to us. We believe that because someone is our wife, daughter, husband, mother, son, father, lover, or friend, that person will think, feel, or act in a certain way. When it doesn't happen, we often become angry.

We may be missing out on happier relationships by choosing our assumptions over reality. Only by letting go of our assumptions about others can we become open to who they really are.

I let go of my assumptions and allow others to show me who they are.

Forgiveness

It is sometimes very difficult to forgive others we feel have wronged us in some way. We may not want to give up our anger. We may feel that justice was never served, that we were never even asked for forgiveness.

But judgments against others reflect judgments we harbor against ourselves. And the anger we carry around turns back on us.

Forgiving others releases us all. In forgiving others, we forgive ourselves. We acknowledge our imperfection and humanity. In this way, we help others become their best selves by freeing them of guilt, shame, fear, and defensiveness.

We don't have to condone or approve of others' behavior to forgive them. We just recognize their humanity and our own.

I forgive and release everyone in my life.

Listening

Sometimes we work so hard at getting our point across to others that we can't hear what they have to say. Sometimes we believe we already know what they think or feel and what they're going to say. Sometimes we only hear their words and not their message.

To be open to receiving another's message, we have to quiet not just our mouths, but also our minds. We have to open not only our ears, but also our hearts.

We can think of every communication from others as either expressions of love or cries for love. If we remember this when we listen to others, we can agree or disagree, take responsibility for ourselves, and say what we need to say. And we can do it with a truer understanding of and respect for others.

I quiet my mind and open my heart to hearing the messages of others.

Self-Righteousness

We may feel powerful and justified in our judgments and our anger toward others. To Let Go and Let God may seem weak or irresponsible to us in many cases. But when it is the hardest for us to let go, it is probably the most important.

Letting go and trusting God, we can turn over our power struggles and discover relief. It is better to find serenity than to be right. It is better to be peaceful than to be right. It is better to remain calm than to be right. As soon as we let go of our need to be right, we discover the joy of being calm, peaceful, and serene.

Our Higher Power is always ready to help us, to take over our struggles. Being right doesn't bring us happiness—calmness, peacefulness, and serenity do.

My recovery depends on letting go of my self-righteousness. I accept peace over the illusion of power.

Compassion

Sometimes we find ourselves with people who seem to wallow in self-pity. They may complain over and over about the same things happening to them. They may have all kinds of excuses for not changing themselves and their lives.

In the past, we may have taken on the feelings and problems of people like this. We may have tried to fix things for them, or tell them what they should do. After we gave up our caretaking behavior, we may have adopted the opposite extreme, refusing to "get involved" by even listening to their stories.

We can find a balance between taking over others and pushing them away. We can see them as reflections of ourselves, and remember to avoid our own self-pity and resistance to change. We can listen to them without involving ourselves in their problems.

I will look upon others with compassion.

Safe Relationships

As we move forward in our growth and development, our old relationships change. While we make the changes needed, it can be very helpful to have one or more safe relationships.

A safe relationship is one where we can be ourselves, be honest, try new behaviors, and make some mistakes. We can have a safe relationship with a therapist or counselor, or with a trusted friend.

Even in a safe relationship, we may get our feelings hurt or be told something that's hard for us to hear. But in a safe relationship, we know we will never be *harmed*. Our confidences will be kept, our feelings will not be ignored, and our well-being will be valued.

These relationships can help us take our first, scary steps toward new ways of interacting with others. And we can remember that our safest relationship of all is with our Higher Power.

I will take advantage of the growth available to me in safe relationships.

Powerlessness

How wonderful the world would be if everyone would just think, feel, and act the way we want them to! This thought, in various forms, may dance about in our minds, even after we think we have accepted our powerlessness. We know we can't control others, but we may still think, *Wouldn't it be nice if...*

We aren't powerless over other people as some kind of punishment. If people only did what we wanted, how could they explore their own development in their own way and time? How could we each find a relationship with our Higher Power? How could we evolve to our highest potential?

We can truly accept our powerlessness and allow others to find their own paths by remembering that we don't know what's best for them.

I accept that my powerlessness over others is for the best.

Harmony

Learning to get along well with others enhances our own lives. We have to deal with other people daily in many ways. If these interactions are harmonious, our lives are easier and happier.

But harmony with others doesn't mean we always have to agree with them or give in to their demands. We aren't required to "keep the peace" at any cost. We can be calm yet assertive, cooperative yet self-directed, respecting each other's individuality while working toward compromise.

In music, harmony isn't everyone singing or playing exactly the same notes at the same time. The beautiful sounds of a symphony orchestra or a barbershop quartet are achieved when all the distinctly different parts are played together. With our Higher Power as conductor, we can achieve a splendid harmony with everyone around us.

Directed by my Higher Power, I play my part in harmony with others.

Maturity

Accepting the things we cannot change, including other people, does *not* mean accepting their abuse. Maturity does *not* mean becoming selfless victims of others.

As we mature through the program, we grow to understand that accepting others as they are also means taking responsibility for ourselves. When we realize that an addict, alcoholic, or abusive person in our lives is not going to change, we must decide what we need to do for our own well-being. Then we must back ourselves up with positive action.

Mature relationships are based on mutual respect, trust, and equality with give and take on both sides. There is caring, understanding, nurturing, and detachment. There is love, and there is also self-love.

I accept others and take responsibility for myself.

Anger

Melody Beattie wrote in *Codependent No More*, "Unpleasant feelings are like weeds. They don't go away when we ignore them; they grow wild and take over."

We may have relationships that have been completely taken over by anger. We can heal ourselves by recognizing our anger and dealing with it appropriately. We can talk about it, write about it, examine our thinking about it, and accept it. Then we can decide what, if anything, needs to be done.

Our anger may be covering up guilt, sadness, hurt, or fear. It may indicate our need to ask for what we want. When we deal with the underlying beliefs and feelings, we can stop blaming others and take responsibility for our anger.

I accept my anger and deal with it appropriately.

Tolerance

According to the dictionary, *tolerance* means accepting others' views, beliefs, and practices without prejudice. It means that the views, beliefs, and practices of others don't have to change or threaten our own. It means not allowing ourselves to be affected negatively by others' choices, but recognizing that they are not *our* choices.

We can all have different opinions, likes and dislikes, beliefs, and ways of living, and that's okay. Intolerance comes from feeling that everyone must agree with us or do things our way. It is a controlling position that grows out of fear and defensiveness.

We can accept others as they are, whether or not they agree with us or behave as we wish. When we take care of ourselves, the differences between us cannot hurt us.

I accept others as they are, without allowing them to harm me.

Faith

Some other people may not handle their lives or problems very well. They may repeat self-defeating patterns and resist change. They may choose to continue addictive behaviors, even after they recognize them or get some treatment. But these are not our problems.

We can remain detached from other people's problems by remembering that our Higher Power works in their lives as well as our own. Whatever another's problems look like to us, they are in the hands of God and that person. Our faith can help us to accept our powerlessness over other people's lives and problems.

Faith doesn't mean that we have to belong to a church or follow any religious tradition. It simply means remembering that there is a Higher Power that can help us all.

My Higher Power can take over other people's problems.

Equality

As our self-image changes, so does our view of others. Nearly everything we have learned about ourselves applies to other people. None of us is able to control others. None of us can change the past or affect the future by worrying about it. All of us are responsible for taking care of ourselves. All of us can get the help we need from our Higher Power.

We are growing in our understanding of ourselves and our Higher Power. We have let go of false beliefs we held about ourselves. We have given up self-defeating attitudes and behaviors.

It doesn't matter whether others believe as we do. Just as we can't choose their path, they can't choose ours. They are like us, and we are like them. We are all human beings doing the best we can right now.

I see others as equal to me.

Sharing

As codependents, we may need to learn what and how much we can share with others. In the past, we may have refused to share at all or put ourselves in danger by sharing too much.

Accepting others as they are means facing the truth about them. If some people don't repay their debts or can't keep a secret, we accept that this is the way they are and we can't change them. But we don't lend them money or tell them secrets.

Sharing is part of relationships. We share our time, feelings, ideas, information about ourselves, and, sometimes, our material things or money. But we must determine the amount and kind of sharing that is appropriate in each case. We can do this by remembering to see and accept others as they are.

I can share with others without allowing myself to be harmed.

Chill Out

We sometimes find ourselves confronted with other people's misplaced anger, criticism, or negativity. Even if we are working our program and feeling good about ourselves, such an attack can plunge us into self-doubt, guilt, fear, anger, or despair.

We need to remember that others also have old negative programming and sometimes act out self-defeating thoughts and beliefs. To diffuse such a confrontation, we can recognize what's really happening. We can examine whether the situation at hand is creating the feelings we both have, or if old tapes are playing.

We can put off our immediate reaction and take the time to *chill out*. We can let go without reacting. We can accept that the other person has old tapes to deal with, and we don't have to respond with ours.

I accept other people's need to deal with their negative programming, but I won't let them trigger mine.

Blame

As we learn to take responsibility for ourselves, we may uncover some old beliefs that others are to blame for all of our problems. We may think that if only we'd had different parents or had never met or become involved with certain people, we wouldn't have developed our codependent behavior. Even if that's true, what difference does it make now?

Blaming is a way of staying bogged down in the past. It's magical thinking to fantasize about how perfect we would be if only others in our lives had been more perfect. Life must be lived in the present. Blame avoids taking responsibility for ourselves and dealing with our problems now.

When we accept the reality of the past and let it go, we can begin to let go of blaming attitudes. Then we can live in the present.

I let go of blaming others for my problems.

Sharing Our Needs

In the past, we may have expected others to rescue us, to fulfill our needs without even asking them. We may not even have known what our needs were, but wanted them to be magically met by others. When this didn't happen, we may have felt disappointed or angry.

Now we are learning to take care of ourselves. We are sorting out our needs and finding out which ones we can meet on our own. We are also discovering what we need from others.

Other people don't automatically know what we need from them even if they love us. When we have sorted it out in our own minds, we need to share this information with others, as clearly and accurately as we can. We can't expect others to fulfill our legitimate needs in a relationship unless we tell them what those needs are.

I share my needs with those close to me.

Grown-Up Babies

A newborn infant gets needs and desires met by crying, which brings someone who can help.

We may treat some adults in our lives as helpless babies. We respond to their "crying" by taking responsibility for their needs, desires, whims, obligations, and happiness. An infant grows more independent over time, but it seems that the more we do for grown-up babies, the less they try to do for themselves.

As we grow more responsible for ourselves and let go of our caretaking behaviors, the "babies" in our lives may cry louder and longer. They may react to our letting go with tantrums or manipulative ploys to make us take care of them again.

We can understand their resistance to take responsibility for themselves, possibly for the very first time. But we must remain committed to our own growth.

I let go of feeling responsible for the grown-up babies in my life.

In Another's Shoes

There is an old saying about not judging others until we've walked a mile in their shoes. We may look at others and believe that, in their place, we would do things differently. But the truth is that if we were actually in their place—with their background and experiences, and their physical, chemical makeup—we'd behave exactly as they do.

It's easy to look around and imagine that we have all the answers for everyone else. But we can never really know what it's like to be in other people's shoes. They are probably doing the best they can at this moment.

As we understand more about our attitudes and behaviors, we can understand others better. We can let go of judging them and concentrate on our growth and development.

I let go of judging others, since I can never really walk in their shoes.

Commitment

We may hold back from fully committing ourselves in relationships. We may set impossibly high expectations of others, and when they fail to meet our standards of perfection, we may quickly end the relationship.

Our difficulty with commitment may rest on a belief, conscious or unconscious, that others can't be trusted. We may expect that sooner or later, we will be hurt. So, to protect ourselves, we just don't become too emotionally involved. We build failure into our relationships.

Commitment in relationships means having realistic expectations, and accepting our own and others' imperfections. It means sometimes compromising and sometimes just accepting differences. It means being able to take the risk of trusting others, because we're also committed to taking care of ourselves.

I can fully commit in relationships without losing myself.

Another title that will interest you...

Codependent No More
by Melody Beattie

The definitive book about codependency, *Codependent No More* is for everyone who has suffered the torment of loving too much. Melody Beattie explains what codependency is, what it isn't, who's got it, and how to move beyond it. This book will be a boon to your self-esteem. 208 pp.
Order No. 5014

Hazelden
Publishing

hazelden.org/bookstore
800-328-9000